SCORPIO

23 OCT–21 NOV

DEREK & JULIA PARKER

A MITCHELL BEAZLEY/MAYFLOWER BOOK

Astrology is a complex science. But that doesn't mean it can't also be fun: and that's the aim of the Zodiac Library! A professional astrologer will look at this series of books rather as a nuclear scientist looks at a mathematical primer. A full Birth Chart (a map of the sky drawn for the moment and from the place of an individual's birth) will contain all the signs of the Zodiac, and the professional astrologer will study these and the positions of the Sun and planets within them, as well as many other factors, before committing himself; so don't expect to recognize all your characteristics in a simple description of your Sun-sign.

We hope this series of books will be a jumping-off place for a study of the complete science of astrology, which is more complicated, much more fascinating, and even more fun than Sun-sign astrology!

Derek and Julia Parker

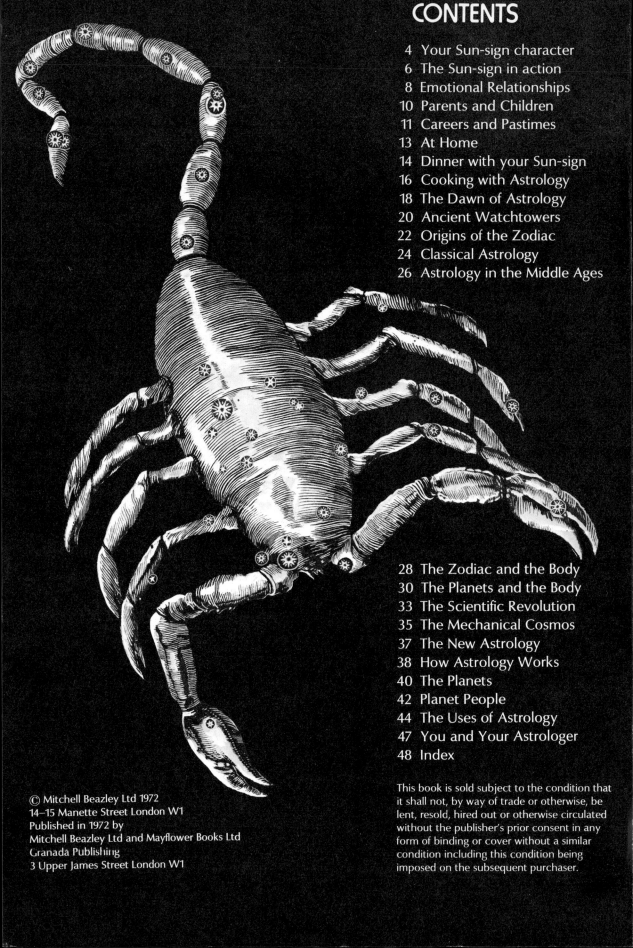

CONTENTS

© Mitchell Beazley Ltd 1972
14–15 Manette Street London W1
Published in 1972 by
Mitchell Beazley Ltd and Mayflower Books Ltd
Granada Publishing
3 Upper James Street London W1

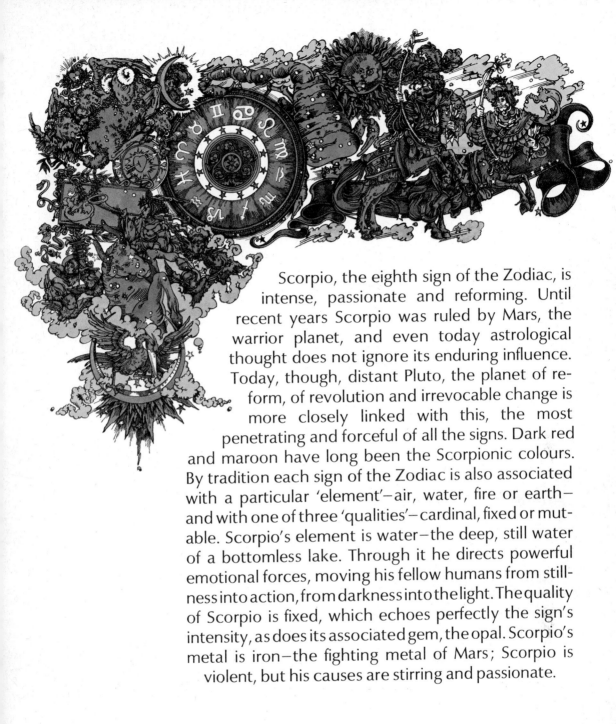

Scorpio, the eighth sign of the Zodiac, is intense, passionate and reforming. Until recent years Scorpio was ruled by Mars, the warrior planet, and even today astrological thought does not ignore its enduring influence. Today, though, distant Pluto, the planet of reform, of revolution and irrevocable change is more closely linked with this, the most penetrating and forceful of all the signs. Dark red and maroon have long been the Scorpionic colours. By tradition each sign of the Zodiac is also associated with a particular 'element'—air, water, fire or earth—and with one of three 'qualities'—cardinal, fixed or mutable. Scorpio's element is water—the deep, still water of a bottomless lake. Through it he directs powerful emotional forces, moving his fellow humans from stillness into action, from darkness into the light. The quality of Scorpio is fixed, which echoes perfectly the sign's intensity, as does its associated gem, the opal. Scorpio's metal is iron—the fighting metal of Mars; Scorpio is violent, but his causes are stirring and passionate.

'Astrology produces joy by anticipation at the same time that it fortifies people against evil.'
Lucian of Samosata (AD 121–181)

YOUR SUN-SIGN CHARACTER

The Zodiacal Self Revealed

The most overwhelming characteristics of Scorpio are his intensity and sense of purpose. To delve deeply— this is the aim by which he is driven in every situation. He cannot skim the surface, whether he is preparing for a university degree or simply reading the Sunday newspapers; the pitch of intensity at which he must live simply will not allow it.

In every description of Scorpio there is an emphasis on passion. This is not only the passion of love: Scorpio has powerful feelings, and will express himself passionately in whatever he is doing. He must live his life at a high emotional level. If he does not, he all too easily becomes resentful and brooding, and his highly charged feelings will remain imprisoned within him rather than be positively expressed.

At such times Scorpio can run into trouble. He may feel that he is unfulfilled or dissatisfied with life. He must then be made aware that such moods may occur, but that they can be prevented so long as he does not repress his *true* feelings. Psychological upsets can be especially damaging to Scorpios.

From a practical point of view, how he directs his emotions is of course a matter for him to decide; but he may well, for instance, feel very strongly about social injustice, bad housing conditions or financial exploitation; it is in areas of this kind that the Scorpio will show up evil, indeed root it out from the dingiest corners.

SIGN OF THE DETECTIVE

It is good for Scorpios to have some 'cause', something in which they can fully immerse themselves, channelling all their powerful feelings positively; and, if they want to, stirring others into action. The Scorpio is a natural detective, and is in his element bringing things into the open. This is a valuable outlet for his energies.

The Scorpio works hard and plays hard. He is no middle-of-the-road man—or girl, for that matter! Overindulgence is something that needs conscious control, but this will be a never-ending battle with him, as he finds restraint difficult. If, on the other hand, he swings too near to excess, the only practical answer is to take drastic remedial action. For instance, if Scorpio discovers he is overweight—this is quite likely from time to time—he must go off to a health farm and live on lemon juice for two weeks. On his first night out afterwards, he may want to celebrate his freedom; but this, to those who know him, is only a first step to new heights of excess, leading him back to the health farm. That's how the Scorpio pendulum swings!

Scorpio's worst fault is his jealousy. Conquering it will not be easy, but he must learn to put up a fight whenever he feels its pangs boiling up inside him. As with all negative traits, recognition is a vital step towards victory.

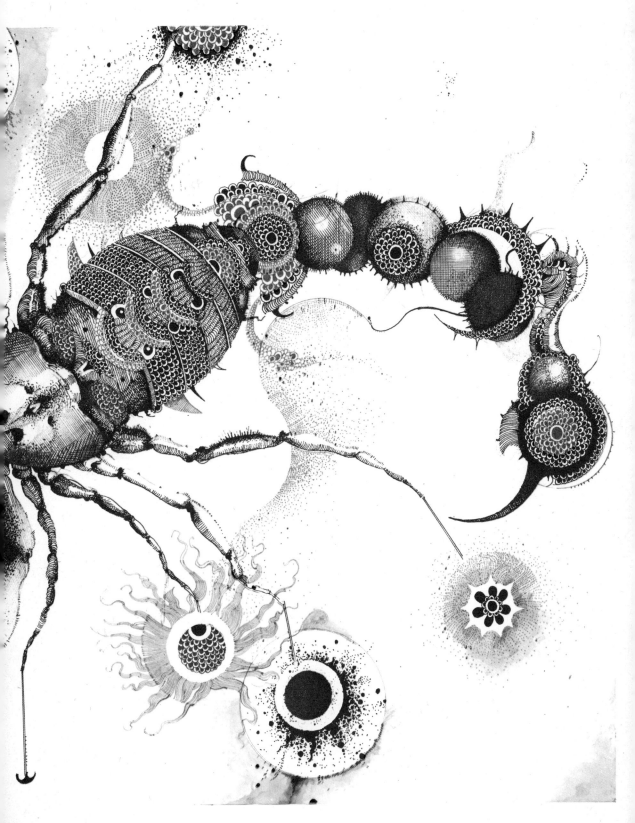

SCORPIO IN ACTION

Mind and Body: You and Your Life Style

Scorpio has magnetic charm: others cannot help but be attracted. This is one of the good-looking signs of the Zodiac, in a dark, intense way. The Scorpio girl may well have a passionate, gypsy air about her, while the man's look is hypnotic and piercing. Both seem to have a special and very individual power, which will come to their aid in any situation, and be used either for good or evil.

The Scorpio seeks to give his life a definite pattern. He will work extremely hard to achieve his ambitions—then quite suddenly will abandon everything and start again from nothing. He will more than likely do this several times during his life. It seems that this pattern of drastic change is necessary to his psychological well-being, and it is expressed not only in his career, but often in his personal life too. There is perhaps a connection here with his intensity: like a volcano he has to erupt from time to time—and will feel all the better for it!

The Scorpio has an enormously high energy level. He is rather like a powerful engine which will deteriorate if left idle. If Scorpio's energy is not burned up it may turn sour on him and he may then fall into a poor physical state; it is possible, too, that he may become a victim of mental distress. The Scorpio cannot be bothered with trivialities, and if he finds that he is involved in work which seems to him to be unimportant, or if he thinks that he is simply a small, rather unnecessary cog in a large wheel, he simply won't function properly. He will feel that the energy he is using is being wasted. Then the rot will set in—and will continue until he decides to make an important change of direction, and sweeps all aside to start anew.

STING IN THE TAIL

Much is written about Scorpionic cruelty—the sting in the tail! Certainly this cannot be ignored, for when Scorpio hurts, he really hurts; and if someone hurts him in return he will not forget it in a hurry. But, strange though it may seem, he may then respond by goading the other person to repeat his action. This is because the Scorpio can, in certain circumstances, be something of a masochist: the worse he is treated the more he will take. But the next time he erupts, he will do so with an explosion that will really shake those who have watched him suffer.

Scorpio rules the genitals, so this area of the body is most susceptible to influence, therefore vulnerable. Scorpio is the most potent of all the signs, and such energy, which can be highly intense, may lead to extreme behaviour; so much so that Scorpios may be roused to act with violence, cruelty, even with sadism. They should recognize this lurking power in themselves, the better to control it.

THE MIND—INTENSE AND CREATIVE

The Scorpio mind, like the whole Scorpio personality, is steeped in intensity. 'Still waters run deep' is perhaps a good way to describe his mental attitude. Scorpios are imaginative but cannot easily make their imaginations work for them. Because the mind is so intense, it is not always easy to prompt it to flow positively. When it does, however, there is a wealth of creative artistic ability to be expressed. If the Scorpio can find a proper outlet, he may contribute a great deal to the world, and in so doing improve his own life. The Scorpio might, for example, do worse than try his hand at crime or detective fiction, for this is one area in which he could excel.

All too often the Scorpio's imagination works overtime—but to frustrate its owner rather than to benefit him. Some strange idea may enter his head—put there, perhaps, by a friend's casual remark. The friend may say he saw Scorpio's wife waiting in a restaurant. Scorpio didn't know she was going out that day. She must be meeting . . . and within minutes he has mentally lined up the whole divorce proceedings—and started to look hard at the girl in the outer office! Unfortunately, too, he will not clear the air immediately he arrives home, but will wait, brooding for a long while before mentioning his fears. And when he does, he will really let fly!

NO STONE UNTURNED

Scorpio is often known as 'the investigator', and can turn his mind to working on the smallest, most complicated area of a big problem. His ability to leave no stone unturned gives him obsessional tendencies, and he can easily become bogged down by his problems. He needs to make sure that this trait does not get the better of him. He has excellent reasoning powers, and these should in most cases see him through his difficulties. His sense of perception is excellent, and provided he can keep a clear perspective he will come to terms with the deeper, darker areas of his mind.

Even so, a measure of conflict may be unavoidable. This is because the Scorpio is inclined to attack all his tasks with an intensity that more easy-going signs may find ferocious and rather frightening.

When Scorpio has a problem, he is inclined to involve himself in analyzing his reactions to it rather than concentrating on the problem itself. This can be a fruitless occupation in some respects: he may gain in self-knowledge, but it will not solve his immediate difficulties. Scorpios are enormously intuitive, and it is to their advantage to use this gift. If they feel that something is wrong, or that some unexpected event is going to take place, they will invariably be on the right track—like the shrewd detectives they are!

EMOTIONAL RELATIONSHIPS

Couples: How You Compare in Friendship, Love and Marriage

SCORPIO IN LOVE

The Scorpio in love is extremely passionate. He will experience many deeply emotional relationships, each more meaningful than the last; and he will not forget past loves in a hurry. They will linger in his mind long after the farewells have been said.

The most common reason for farewells in the Scorpio's love-life is his sometimes violent jealousy. Some partners cannot cope with this; and unless they have a great deal of inner strength they may not put up with it for long. It will be the cause, too, of some hard-hitting quarrels. Unfortunately it is hard for the Scorpio to realize how potent and completely negative his jealous attitude really is.

Scorpio is an attentive escort: only the best restaurants, the best hotels will be good enough; he will certainly see to it that the setting is exactly right for his big seduction scene! Obviously, he is an expert, and the girl of his affections will be fascinated, slightly scared and completely magnetized by his approach! If Scorpio can manage to keep his jealousy at bay, then the affair could hit the high spots.

SCORPIO AND HIS FRIENDS

The Scorpio friend will be demanding, and those with a less powerful energy-level may struggle to keep up with his searching questions, his constant demands for their opinions, and his strong feelings on everything from the latest big fight to the next election results. He will always want to pursue a subject in great depth;

	Aries	Taurus	Gemini	Cancer	Leo	Virgo
Friendship	Good, but stormy: if you want a relaxing evening, don't telephone your Arian friend.	Good. They have qualities you admire; you can both get angry but the friendship should be stable and long-lived.	Not easy, but you might steady Gemini's jumpy ways and make him more consistent.	Quite good, but Cancerians may be just a little too sentimental for you.	If you can really let Leo be king of the castle all will be well – but can you?	Excellent, how you will love going over the tiny details together. Your plans should never go astray, you are both too careful.
Love Life	Scorpion meets Ram. Passionate, you may never go out, but spiky too.	Taurus, although passionate, may be slow to respond to you. Take your time – it will be worthwhile!	Gemini may well have another relationship going; if you are jealous this will only make them look for a third!	Emotions will run high; they are very sensitive and you can be cruel at times. Take care.	'A good time all round – here's someone who appreciates your taste for living it up; this one could be expensive, if anyone's counting.	Virgoans are extremely choosy and clinical, you are extra sensual – which could cause a lot of trouble.
Marriage	You will both fight for your highly potent marriage: control your jealous instinct.	Excellent if you remember that your worst fault is jealousy and theirs is being possessive.	Gemini is a mental lightweight, and you are a 'heavy', a prober; this needs understanding.	A sympathetic pairing if you do not trample on their sensitivity – and get your head bitten off in return.	Colourful and rarely dull, but remember you are both emotional in different ways. You brood then explode, Leo just explodes.	You both work hard, but may get on each other's nerves. If in difficulty look to your love life for explanations.

obviously, from a friend's point of view, it is advisable to confine such discussions to common ground. Scorpio is usually a big spender, and will not worry if his friend is less well-off. He is generous to a fault, and loves to spread his money around: he does this not to buy popularity, but simply because he likes life, and wants others to do so. Even in friendship, however, jealousy can occur, and tact is sometimes needed to prevent Scorpio's emotions from boiling over.

MARRIAGE – THE FACTS

In marriage, Scorpio's potency needs to find a satisfactory outlet. This is essential, because he is so highly powered. Otherwise he will become restless, and will soon look for relationships outside marriage. Anyone

contemplating marriage with a Scorpio should realize that it will be no wishy-washy affair, grey or colourless; this partnership will be bold and bright, filled with striking contrasts of happiness and moments of near-despair, or worse. The husband or wife of a Scorpio will have to work at the part, for it is a double one of husband-lover or wife-mistress. That is the challenge. The reward – though there will be great dramas, and plates may fly – is a colourful, passionate partnership.

Below: Use this Friends and Lovers Sun-sign chart to check how Scorpio is likely to make out with others in friendship, love and marriage. Relationships are listed from left to right, Scorpio to Aries, Scorpio to Taurus, etc., and from top to bottom in friendship, love and marriage.

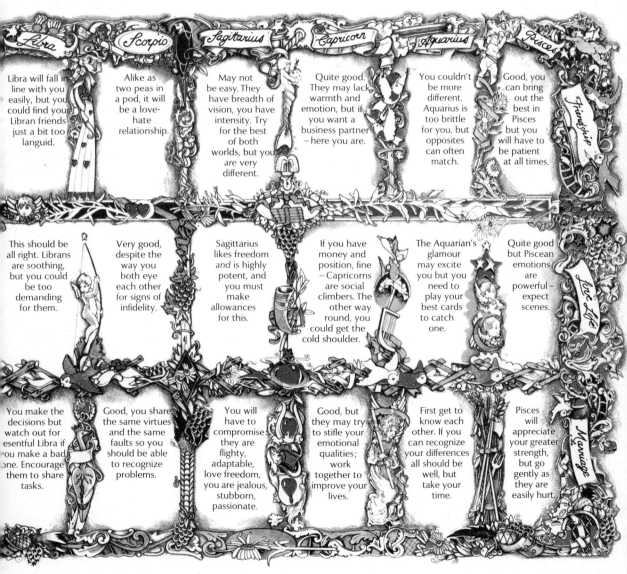

Libra	Scorpio	Sagittarius	Capricorn	Aquarius	Pisces	
Libra will fall in line with you easily, but you could find your Libran friends just a bit too languid.	Alike as two peas in a pod, it will be a love-hate relationship.	May not be easy. They have breadth of vision, you have intensity. Try for the best of both worlds, but you *are* very different.	Quite good. They may lack warmth and emotion, but if you want a business partner – here you are.	You couldn't be more different. Aquarius is too brittle for you, but opposites can often match.	Good, you can bring out the best in Pisces but you will have to be patient at all times.	Friendship
This should be all right. Librans are soothing, but you could be too demanding for them.	Very good, despite the way you both eye each other for signs of infidelity.	Sagittarius likes freedom *and* is highly potent, and you must make allowances for this.	If you have money and position, fine – Capricorns are social climbers. The other way round, you could get the cold shoulder.	The Aquarian's glamour may excite you but you need to play your best cards to catch one.	Quite good but Piscean emotions are powerful – expect scenes.	Love Life
You make the decisions but watch out for resentful Libra if you make a bad one. Encourage them to share tasks.	Good, you share the same virtues and the same faults so you should be able to recognize problems.	You will have to compromise; they are flighty, adaptable, love freedom, you are jealous, stubborn, passionate.	Good, but they may try to stifle your emotional qualities; work together to improve your lives.	First get to know each other. If you can recognize your differences all should be well, but take your time.	Pisces will appreciate your greater strength, but go gently as they are easily hurt.	Marriage

9

PARENTS AND CHILDREN

The Zodiac Family Portrait

THE SCORPIO FATHER

When a Scorpio becomes a father, he will feel a burst of pride and will throw himself ardently into his new role. Later on he should take care that he is not too strict; he has this tendency, and a sensitive child, perhaps a girl, could become rather afraid of him. He may find this difficult to believe, for he probably feels that his bark is worse than his bite; in reality, though, this may not be strictly true. However, the feminine charm of his little girl will go straight to his heart, and she, if she inherits her father's subtlety, should find it easy enough to win him round to her way of thinking!

The Scorpio father will be equally strict with his sons; but they will probably be quite tough in their own ways, and could well thrive on a direct, straightforward approach. The Scorpio father will plan marvellous outings from time to time, and these will help to make him popular with his children. But tolerance is one important lesson all Scorpios have to learn, *especially* when they become fathers.

THE SCORPIO MOTHER

The Scorpio mother will probably throw herself as passionately into the idea of motherhood as she entered her husband's arms on their wedding night! She will in most cases be a very good mother. Strictness may be a problem with her, as with the Scorpio father, but her maternal pride may help her to keep a balance.

She could at times become rather too demanding. On the other hand Scorpio's great energy and flair for enjoying life will give the children plenty of splendid memories as they grow older; whether the family is rich or poor, time must be made for fun. Scorpios tend to be fixed in their opinions, and as the children grow up the parents may forget to keep abreast of the younger generation's opinions. Scorpio parents must resolve really to *do* something about the generation gap – or it could cause more difficulties than usual.

THE SCORPIO CHILD

The Scorpio child needs a great deal of careful up-bringing and guidance, and strict discipline. He will have a strong personality and be determined, even quite stubborn at times. All his searching questions must be answered in detail, and parents will do well not to gloss over facts. Scorpio children need to get the facts straight, and if their parents do not supply them, they will try to find out in their own way – which could produce strange, perhaps unhappy results.

The Scorpio child loves mystery, and once he has reached the reading age will devour quantities of mystery stories – the creepier the better! He will tend to be secretive, and this trait must be watched with considerable care. It can, however, be developed positively if, for instance, the young Scorpio is entrusted with planning birthday surprises and 'secrets' for other members of the family.

Unfortunately, the great Scorpio green-eyed monster – jealousy – is certain to show its head, especially when a younger brother or sister is born into the family and begins to make his or her presence felt. But if the Scorpio child can be made to feel really wanted, and is made responsible for looking after the baby in some way, this will help. But he *must* afterwards be rewarded with great praise and affection. He will probably be an energetic child, and should be encouraged to take part in all the heavier sports. He should also learn to swim very early in life (water is his element); later he could take to underwater swimming and perhaps to skiing, either on water or snow. He will be one of the world's workers, and with encouragement will work hard at school. At the same time he may mislead teachers into thinking that he knows less than he actually does. A slightly cruel streak in him will enjoy watching the poor teacher trying to explain something to him in many different ways, when all the time he knows exactly what she means!

If the question of a boarding school arises for the Scorpio child, generally speaking he should respond well to the life. He can take the additional discipline and will soon find his own individual ways of enjoying life. His midnight feasts will not be discovered (he will, already, be a skilled secret agent) and the food he organizes will be excellent! However, all Scorpio children need care in their upbringing. They have enormously strong characters, and any negative tendencies should be checked at once or they may persist in adult life, perhaps with unfortunate consequences.

GEMINI. Always active with many irons in the fire, but needs encouragement to complete tasks.

LIBRA. Finds decision-making difficult. Help to combat this weakness during early years, or life may be difficult later.

PISCES. Needs help to develop strength of character. Powerful emotions and imagination seek positive outlet, perhaps through art.

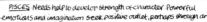

SAGITTARIUS. Needs freedom, open air, dislikes restrictive discipline, cramped surroundings. Excellent mental powers, open to reason.

CAPRICORN. Tends to be a loner, loves reading, can do well in athletics, climbing. Encourage to realise ambitions.

CANCER. Naturally protective especially towards younger brothers and sisters; should try to broaden horizons.

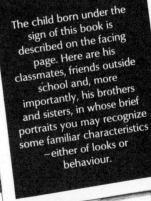

TAURUS. Has a sweet tooth, parents should control candy intake; likely to put on weight.

VIRGO. Always ready to help clean and tidy; school problems may cause digestive upsets, encourage open discussion.

The child born under the sign of this book is described on the facing page. Here are his classmates, friends outside school and, more importantly, his brothers and sisters, in whose brief portraits you may recognize some familiar characteristics —either of looks or behaviour.

AQUARIUS. Naturally independent, can seem eccentric at times, but has a deeply humanitarian spirit. Friendly though unemotional.

LEO. Good organiser, likes to be in charge. Tends to show off, but natural spirit must not be crushed.

ARIES. Enjoys sport, keen to take the lead, but accident-prone and suffers cuts and bruises.

CAREERS AND PASTIMES
A Sun-sign Guide to Work and Play

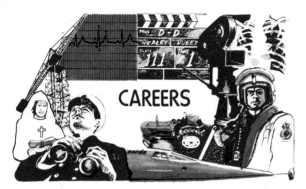

CAREERS

Scorpios are hard workers, and their sense of purpose in life makes them serious in their approach to a career. They have the ability to study hard during training, whether at university or college, or in some form of apprenticeship or articles. Their determination, whatever their level of intelligence or type of job, should help them to make good progress. However, they must feel that their work is important. They hate trivialities. Scorpios have excellent business sense, and will be happy in insurance, the Stock Exchange, or working for any large business concern.

They are great researchers, and have the ability to bring out into the open that which is concealed: and many Scorpios are compulsively drawn to criminal investigation and the police force. Very often they find themselves fighting their own kind, for some Scorpio traits can be expressed, negatively, through crime.

We can of course take this theme further, for the spying profession seems to hold everything that a Scorpio needs for a satisfactory life! In addition to the attractions already mentioned, there is danger—extreme danger—which is just what Scorpio will thrive on. Although he is not reckless or foolhardy, he will be immensely stimulated by the idea of living on a razor's edge.

The Scorpio would also make an excellent psychiatrist or analyst. He is able to reveal and disentangle the complexities of the human mind. He can also turn his attention profitably to surgery, which he will perform with infinite, delicate skill. It is perhaps in this profession that the Scorpio is really at his best, using all his powerful qualities to the utmost.

The Scorpio not only likes administering discipline, but responds to it himself: it is, however, the discipline of action, of additional work and of energy expended, not the discipline of restriction, confinement or repression. He makes an ideal soldier, for he is so tough and such a strong personality that even if he advances in the ranks, which is very likely, he will inflict a strict discipline on himself to 'lead by example', as he would

say. Nevertheless, his motivations are not always so straightforward: he may inflict discipline because of his own masochistic liking for it! Both the Army and the Navy are excellent for Scorpio.

In choosing a career, Scorpio must at all times remember his need to stretch himself to the limits if he is to find satisfaction in his work. He must not only work hard, he must be able to exercise his inquiring mind, and above all else he must feel strongly that what he is doing is important to the community as a whole, and to himself in particular.

PASTIMES

As the Scorpio seeks to stretch himself in his career so he needs to in his spare-time, and his interests should act as a dynamic contrast to his working life. For instance, if he has an intellectually demanding job, he should have a physically demanding pastime; or, if the demands at work on his physical energy are heavy, he should exercise his mind to the fullest out of working hours.

Much of the Scorpio's spare time will undoubtedly be taken up with making love, and with improving his techniques. However, he has many other talents which could also be a great source of pleasure to him! As he has a high energy level, some form of sporting activity will please him. He may well go in for team games—either to play or watch. Boxing could attract him from an early age, and he will also be excellent at karate. It might be extremely good for him from a psychological point of view to have an outlet of this kind. He is aggressive, and a semi-violent hobby will help him to work it out of his system.

Scorpio is often attracted to swimming, and to some of the more challenging water sports, such as water-skiing, or perhaps under-water exploration. Indeed, any activity which entails a certain amount of risk will fascinate Scorpios—both men and girls. They will very likely be attracted to sailing, for example—but the exciting, dangerous sport of large racing craft, rather than peaceful river cruising.

AT HOME

A Sun-sign Guide to Home Décor

Exotic shades of red will dominate the Scorpio's taste in decoration. The carpets will be thick, luxurious and probably maroon; quite often black will also be used. The atmosphere might, to others, seem rather claustrophobic: and the general impression will certainly be seductive! There will be low, relaxing couches with plenty of soft, comfortable cushions. These are likely to be patterned with large tropical blossoms, or some sort of mystical Eastern design; again, the effect is mainly sensual and some may find the lack of ambiguity somewhat disconcerting.

The Scorpio may even burn incense, for he is often inclined to the occult, and adores an air of mystery. The lighting will be kept low, and directed to specific areas of the room. Light fittings will tend to be modern and sleek.

Scorpio likes good food, and the dining-area will be emphasized. The dining-table will be in highly polished dark wood, and the chairs will be comfortably upholstered. There is likely to be a special table prominently placed for drinks, for the Scorpio knows his wines and spirits well, and visitors can expect the best available, and plenty of it, too.

PEACOCK FEATHERS OR A CRYSTAL BALL
Some bizarre ornament or item of decoration may add an element of shock, surprise anyway, to the scene,

such as an arrangement of peacock feathers, or unusual artificial flowers. A stuffed alligator or a case of butterflies or insects may slightly startle the visitor – or even a crystal ball!

The Scorpio's taste in pictures is as definite as his whole clear-cut, strong personality. He will love the exotic paintings of Gauguin (especially the Tahitian nudes). He will like Dali's surrealism, and perhaps the weird canvasses of Hieronymus Bosch. Dürer's marvellous knights in armour could well attract him, and if he is a student he will tend to go for posters of exotic nudes, photographs of Indian temple sculpture, or reproductions of equally sensual works by Aubrey Beardsley.

The financially well-established Scorpio will have a slick kind of taste, and may buy pictures for investment; but nevertheless he is unlikely to buy anything he dislikes. Fortunately for him, love and the human body are here to stay, and he can find both investment value and sensual pleasure in many fields of art.

If Scorpio likes pop music, it will probably be the heavier, slower numbers that will appeal to him; generally, on entering the Scorpio home, one can expect lush sounds to strike one's ears. If his taste is classical, it may be the strains of a pulsating rhythm, such as Ravel's *Bolero*, that waft out to greet the visitor in the entrance hall.

DINNER WITH SCORPIO

Entertaining with Your Sun-sign

THE HOST

If a Scorpio invites you to dinner, accept quickly before he changes his mind, because it is likely to be a splendid evening. Scorpios do nothing by halves, and playing the host is an activity they enjoy. They do find trivialities irritating, however, preferring to feel that every occasion in which they involve themselves is important. In some this sense of occasion, coupled perhaps with a wish to influence people, may mean that the visitor will find himself sitting between a senior politician and a bishop. The talk will be spirited, but an argument could quite possibly blow up over the brandy.

THE GUEST

Scorpio guests are always interesting, and have a generally dynamic air. They may, however, be a little suspicious of any new dish they have not tasted before. The best way to comfort Scorpio guests is to appeal to their imagination; this usually induces contentment.

On the other hand, if a dish is *too* successful—especially if it is a dish that your Scorpio guest is in the habit of cooking from time to time—then you may find that paeans of praise from your other guests will awaken his ready sense of jealousy, after which sparks will fly! Scorpio is the legendary lover's sign: and indeed, if you have not planned the splendid meal as a means of seducing him, he might take advantage of it to seduce you!

THE SETTING

Dark red and maroon are the Scorpio colours, perhaps with a small admixture of dark green, together producing an effect that by many standards is rather sombre. As to music, the smoother, more romantic versions of the classic pop songs form the kind of background that Scorpios find sympathetic—Sinatra, Ella Fitzgerald and others—but refer also to page 13 for a general assessment of the Scorpio's musical tastes.

WINES

Scorpio wines present a slight problem: the countries with which Scorpios are particularly associated are Norway and Syria. Syrian wine is on the whole rather rough, and a less seductive drink than *arrack* it would be hard to find! If one were to compromise slightly on the country of origin, then perhaps a Beaune would be ideal. There will also be a yen for the rather pompous kind of drinks—a good old brandy, a sound port, or any bottle with an impressive label on it.

Right: An all-star evening for famous Scorpios of past and present would very likely include all the illustrious guests in our picture (not all, incidentally, believers in astrology!). For details of the various dishes on the table—every one a Scorpio favourite—turn to page 16.

Princess Grace of Monaco

Mrs Indira Ghandi

Viscount Montgomery

Billy Graham   Katharine Hepburn

amein   Pablo Picasso   Field Marshal Erwin Rommel

RECIPES FOR SCORPIO

Cooking with Astrology

Using astrology to choose a menu is something many people do just for fun. Some foods are traditionally associated with certain astrological signs; but, in other cases, we rely on our own researches and experience of the way the Sun-signs react to certain dishes.

Scorpio, for instance, is a water sign, and it is more than likely that clam chowder will intrigue and delight the Scorpio guest. Lobster Newburg has a richness that will satisfy the Scorpio diner – and the difference between a scorpion and a lobster is sufficiently slight to make an interesting comparison. Scorpio colours, dark red and maroon, can be observed in their deepest, most virile tones in the blackcurrant pie.

As for prunes in sherry, well, Scorpios do tend to eat more than is good for them, and the effect of the prune on the digestion is legendary. Of course, cooking with astrology *is* just fun – but it's surprising just how often the theory turns out to be accurate!

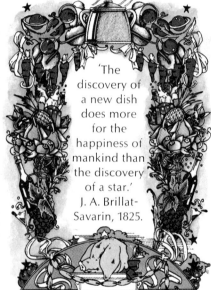

'The discovery of a new dish does more for the happiness of mankind than the discovery of a star.'
J. A. Brillat-Savarin, 1825.

CLAM CHOWDER

You either like shellfish, or you don't; but clam chowder is an excellently 'impressive' dish, and not difficult. Peel and chop 1 large potato; cover with cold water; bring to the boil and drain immediately. Repeat this blanching process with 5 to 6 slices unsmoked bacon, chopped. In a large pan, sauté bacon in butter for a few minutes. Add $\frac{1}{2}$ Spanish onion, finely chopped, and continue to simmer for a few minutes until lightly golden. Add potato, a bay leaf and the juice from a can of clams. While this is simmering for 20 minutes, mince the clams. Add them to the liquid and continue to simmer for a further 15 minutes. Thicken with a little cornflour and season generously with salt and pepper.

PRUNES IN SHERRY

Boil prunes for 15 minutes (in water, not sherry!); then soak them overnight in sweet sherry. Drain and dry prunes; remove stones and stuff prunes with a hot chutney. Wrap each prune in a strip of unsmoked bacon and secure with a wooden (not plastic) cocktail stick. Just before serving, grill until prunes are hot through and bacon lightly crisped.

BOEUF EN CROÛTE

Buy as much beef fillet as you can afford or get away with. Brush it with brandy, first removing all fat, and cover with a mixture of finely chopped and sautéed mushrooms and onion. Place in a 500°F (Mark 9) oven; immediately lower heat to 350°F (Mark 4) and roast for not more than 15 minutes. Cool slightly; then place a thin slice of pâté (classically, de foie) on top and wrap the lot in puff pastry. Glaze with beaten egg and bake in a fairly hot oven (425°F, Mark 7) for 15 minutes, or until pastry is puffed and crisp. Let no one tell you this is not an expensive dish: try it instead with pork fillet smothered with a mixture of chopped mushrooms, onion and parsley – no pâté. Wrap in pastry and bake. Of course, this hasn't the snobbish appeal of the beef, but if anything it's even more delicious.

LOBSTER NEWBURG

Of the many ways of cooking lobster, perhaps this is the most delicious. Boil the beast for 15 minutes; split it in half and remove meat, not forgetting claws. In a pan, heat diced lobster meat gently in 4 tablespoons butter. Stir in $\frac{1}{2}$ teaspoon paprika; add 1 to 2 tablespoons warmed brandy and set alight (a touch of the spectacular if you switch off the lights first). Pour in 1 glass dry sherry – and don't embark on Lobster Newburg unless you have both sherry and brandy! Beat 2 tablespoons double cream lightly with 1 egg yolk. Remove pan from heat and stir in egg mixture gradually. Season with salt and pepper. Return to heat and cook gently, stirring constantly, until sauce and lobster are thoroughly hot again and sauce has thickened. Take great care not to let it boil, or egg yolk will curdle. Serve at once with plain boiled rice. And if your guests don't finish every scrap, don't ask them again.

BLACKCURRANT PIE

Wash about $1\frac{1}{2}$ lb. blackcurrants and put them in a pie dish. Cover with 3 oz brown sugar (more if your tooth is particularly sweet) and moisten with about $\frac{1}{4}$ pint water. Cover pie with shortcrust pastry; brush with cold water and sprinkle top with a little sugar. Bake at 390°F (Mark 5–6) for 25 minutes. Serve either hot or cold, but certainly with plenty of cream.

THE ORIGINS, MEANING AND POWER OF ASTROLOGY

THE DAWN OF ASTROLOGY

Man's First Responses to
Celestial Influence

When the Moon passes across the face of the Sun in a total solar eclipse, even we in the 1970s feel disquiet, a moment of tension. Today the Sun and Moon undoubtedly have a strong physical effect on our lives, and that effect must have been much more strongly sensed in prehistoric times.

For early man, life was often savage and uncomfortable, his struggle to live was assailed by storms, merciless heat, famine, disease, drought. He had, moreover, to beat off attacks on his livestock from wild animals and to withstand the blows that his equally wild human neighbours aimed at his own life. As he hunted, fished, simply attempted to keep himself warm and well fed, he noticed the warmth of the Sun above him and the gradually increased cold as winter came on; the alternation of light and dark and the rhythmic motions of the sea on the shore. His attention was naturally drawn to those bodies in the sky that were constantly on the move against an apparently still background. Those bodies were the Sun, Moon and planets, and they were especially sharp to the eye in Mesopotamian latitudes where the atmosphere was clear and bright and where civilization—and astrology—began.

POWER TO THE PLANETS

The stars and planets offered early man a mirror. In them he saw an upper world that not only reflected his own predicament but—once he could interpret its secrets—would positively guide him through difficult times, avert disasters and set him on the right roads to peace and prosperity.

Almost as far back as records survive we find the notion of the Sun, Moon and planets as personalities, either commanding human life or intervening in it. The Sun and Moon formed a family group with Mercury and Venus (to call them by the well-known names that the Romans later gave them). Mercury and Venus then acquired the reputation of being respectively good and evil. Mars, Jupiter and Saturn made up a rival family with Jupiter at its head; and because Jupiter, as the leader, could only be good, the other two were thought to be evil.

Soon the planets took on more or less fixed characteristics: Mercury, the quick, cunning, fox-like planet-god, became associated with a shrewd kind of wisdom (he also became, incidentally, bisexual); Mars was the ruler of violence and war; Jupiter a king-like ruler of men; Saturn a somewhat cruel, morose god. The Sun, Jupiter and Saturn were particularly active by day, and the Moon, Mars and Venus by night. Men born under their influence, when they occupied certain positions in the sky, were in due course credited with a set of planetary characteristics unique to their time and place of birth.

ANCIENT WATCHTOWERS
The Great Quest Begins to Harness the Upper World

Left and *below:* The Caracol observatory at Chichen Itza, Mexico, where Mayan astrologers studied the planets. Below, on the wedding day of a Mayan city-chief, astrologers watch a favourable star enter their forked stick.

Right: Menhirs or great stones at Carnac, France, once linked with powerful Sun cults.

Far right: At Giza, Egypt, the corridors of the pyramids served as tubes for sighting the stars.

Even the ancients were concerned not only with the positions of the planets as related to the observer's viewpoint on earth, but also with the angular relationships that they appeared to form with each other. The early astronomer-astrologers reasoned that if the planets were to be regarded as human and as sharing human emotions, then they could be expected to have certain effects on each other. Venus and Mercury, for example, would be able to argue with the Sun, and to modify his judgments; neighbours must have some influence on the royal family, and at the same time would tend to quarrel among themselves, taking sides or even making a solitary stand for good or evil.

MOUNDS AND MEGALITHS
However, before the meaning behind the positions taken up by the various planets could be interpreted, it was obviously essential to be able to pinpoint those positions with great accuracy. For detailed work of this kind two principal methods were devised—megaliths and mounds. The huge stones brought to megalithic sites at Stonehenge, Carnac and elsewhere were positioned with almost miraculous precision to record the progressive movements through the year of

various celestial bodies. The 'mound' principle was applied in all kinds of towers, pyramids and other monumental structures offering a broader sweep of horizon; these sometimes contained sloping corridors or specially angled windows that could act as sighting devices. The appearances of particular planets in these apertures were carefully recorded, and from that information celestial maps and calendars were compiled.

It is astonishing indeed to find just how many large-scale structures all over the world, in India, China, Europe, the Middle East and America, were either built as observatories or watchtowers or were in some way adapted to the study of events in the heavens—and principally those occurring around the annual route of the Sun, as viewed from Earth. Around this path, which we now call the ecliptic, lay the region of the Zodiac, that central band of sky containing the star groups from which are derived the twelve astrological signs, which run from Aries to Pisces.

Below: One of the ziggurats or watchtowers of Ur; from these huge structures, Babylonian astrologers first observed that the revolving heavens moved to a pattern, in which lay the key to man's understanding of his earthly world.

ORIGINS OF THE ZODIAC

The Star-gods Take Their Appointed Places

In a Babylonian text, written in about 700 BC, reference is made to the Zodiac belt, and fifteen constellations are described as lying within it. In time the number of 'chief constellations' was reduced to twelve and the Zodiac belt was divided into twelve sections of 30° each. The Sun, which passed through the Zodiac once a year, was then seen to 'dwell' in turn in each sign of the Zodiac for a period of thirty days.

The creatures chosen to represent the constellations were taken from the everyday world of early civilizations in the Mediterranean region, and notably those of Babylonia (including Chaldea) and Assyria. There are seven bestial signs—Aries the Ram, Taurus the Bull, Cancer the Crab, Leo the Lion, Scorpio the Scorpion, Capricorn the Goat (or Sea-goat) and Pisces the Fishes. Four signs are 'human'—Gemini the Twins, Virgo the Virgin, Sagittarius the Archer and Aquarius the Water Carrier. (Although half horse, Sagittarius is judged to be human because of the human *activity*—firing a bow— with which he is associated.) Libra the Scales is neither bestial nor human but is considered to be a 'humane' sign, concerned with justice.

THE HOUSES

As the Earth turned on its axis once in every twenty-four hours so the Sun, Moon and planets were seen by the Chaldeans and other early observers to rise and set within this pattern, the entire sky shifting through one Zodiacal sign (or 30°) every two hours. In conjunction with this daily movement astrologers developed a system of Houses. From the line of the observer's horizon, the celestial globe was divided into twelve sections. Each section represented an area of life, as follows: 1 Life; 2 Poverty/riches; 3 Brothers/sisters; 4 Parents; 5 Children; 6 Health; 7 Husband/wife; 8 Death; 9 Religion; 10 Aspirations; 11 Friendship; 12 Family. The planets were then described in terms of the signs and houses they occupied at the moment of birth and their influence was gauged accordingly.

In their work of documenting the motions of the planets the first astrologers of Babylonia and Assyria saw that events in the sky repeated themselves, and the first tables of planetary movements were drawn up. The earliest recorded ephemerides, as they are called, date from the reign of King Assurbanipal (668–625 BC).

The future the astrologers foretold was usually not that of an individual but of the State. They were quite clear that the heavens and the Earth were interrelated, but they had no evidence that an individual could claim particular planetary influences—except one man, the King, who was seen as the embodiment of the State, and whose birth-time was used for State forecasts. These noted the approach and assessed the likely effects of major events such as famine, war and pestilence.

The Fishes, from a wall painting at Knossos, Crete, the centre of a Bronze Age civilization. In astrology Pisceans often feel driven—like the symbolic fishes— in two directions at the same time.

One of the first Sagittarians—a mythical Centaur, half-man, half-horse, shown trampling a rival to death; from the Elgin Marbles.

Egyptian gods weigh the dead; in Babylonian religion Libra was linked with the judgment of souls.

Above: From Sumeria, a compelling image for primitive Capricornians of a he-goat made of gold and lapis-lazuli. In time Capricorn was established as a fish-tailed goat, known to the ancient Babylonians as Ea, the 'antelope of the subterranean ocean', and as Kusarikku, the fish-ram.

Left: At Karnak, Egypt, where this avenue of figures is situated, the ram-headed sphinx was considered to be a symbol of power, mystery and wisdom.

In every culture the bull was taken up as a symbol of strength, and often of creative energy; this head represents the bull-god of Knossos, Crete.

CLASSICAL ASTROLOGY

*Ancient Egypt, Greece and Rome—A New Age
of Horoscopes for All*

The Egyptians were celebrated scientists and enthusiastic observers of the heavens, producing star charts as long ago as the fifth millenium BC. Their preoccupation with calendar-making and mathematics considerably helped the advance of astrology; the astrological functions of the great pyramids are still being researched today. One of the most famous of the astrologer-kings was Rameses II, 'Ozymandias, King of Kings', whose tomb at his death in *c* 1223 BC was richly decorated with astrological symbols. He it also was who fixed the four cardinal signs—Aries, Libra, Cancer and Capricorn. And from the temple of Denderah a relief, dated at about 30 BC, shows the first pictorial representation of the Zodiac to have survived: more precisely, two Zodiacs are featured, one within the other, principally supported by four standing female figures.

From Egypt too came a group of manuscripts collected under the name of 'Hermes Trismegistus', the founder of a medico-astrological cult. Many of its ingredients were also purely magical, and it is the first concrete example of astrology being linked with the occult; one of the most interesting ideas contained in the manuscripts is that correspondences exist between the great outer world (the macrocosm) and man the microcosm.

ASTROLOGY REACHES THE PEOPLE

The Greeks took to astrology with great enthusiasm, as witness a great number of surviving documents and monuments decorated with astrological symbols. It is from the time of Antiochus of Commene (about 30 BC) that the earliest horoscopes from Greek literary sources survive; from the next five centuries or so, about 180 individual horoscopes have come down to us. The Greeks' great contribution to astrology was in fact to rationalize and popularize it, making birth charts available to all and not just the preserve of the ruler— as representative of the State.

By 280 BC, the Babylonian astrologer Berosus, whose works appeared in Greek libraries, had been able to set up a highly successful school of astrology on the island of Cos, and astrologers were already setting out and rationalizing in textbooks the sum total of all they knew for posterity. This burst of study culminated in the first modern astrological text, the *Tetrabiblos*, attributed to the great astronomer, mathematician and geographer, Claudius Ptolemy. He was born in Greece in about AD 120, and was one of the major thinkers of his time. His work as a geographer and mathematician was thorough and revolutionary, and his *Syntaxis* survived for 1,400 years as the most comprehensive source of Greek astronomical ideas. The *Tetrabiblos* is an extraordinary book, as well argued as many modern textbooks (and better than some); many of its general principles are still accepted today.

SLAVES OF DESTINY: IMPERIAL ROME

During the first two centuries after Christ, astrological activity centred on Imperial Rome. In those days, as soon as it became

Right: The Roman Emperor Augustus (ruled 27 BC– AD 14) bravely risked publishing his horoscope—so revealing the death date predicted for him—and he had a silver coin struck which bore his sign—Capricorn. The sea-goat is shown guiding a small globe, included to symbolize Rome's power in the world.

clear that a man was a candidate for the emperor's throne, astrologers gathered around him. Naturally, the emperors tended to snap up the most convincing, most lucid, most persuasive astrologers available, and then kept them busy around the hub of power – if only to discourage pretenders to the throne. They looked on any attempt by someone else to consult an astrologer as extremely suspect, and as probably indicating a plot to seize power.

Tiberius (reigned AD 14–37) was of all the Roman emperors perhaps the most slavishly addicted to astrology. His accession and 'lofty destiny' had been predicted at his birth, and right until the end of his life – particularly during his retirement at Capri, when his excesses made him one of the most despised, hated and feared of men – he was surrounded by what Juvenal called his 'herd of Chaldeans'.

Claudius I (emperor AD 41–54) was old-fashioned in his ideas and preferred divination by bird-flight (augury) to astrology; indeed, he banned astrologers from the country – although the ban was not very successfully enforced. Later, a noble Roman was caught consulting an astrologer to inquire when Claudius would die – and was himself rewarded with a sudden and violent end.

Nero (AD 54–68), although on the whole disinclined to favour any religion, was excessively superstitious, and was encouraged by his astrologers to perpetrate a number of atrocities. Bilbilus, his official astrologer, advised him to divert the evil effects of a comet by slaughtering the heads of most of the great families of Rome.

THE EMPRESS AND THE GLADIATOR

Later emperors, if occasionally protesting their derisive opinion of old-fashioned superstitions, were careful to keep an astrologer about the house. Vespasian officially exiled all astrologers, but retained the most notable of them to serve him personally. His son Titus consulted foreign astrologers and was a firm believer. Domitian was utterly reliant on his astrologers. He dismissed and even murdered noblemen found in possession of the Imperial horoscope, and carefully studied the birth charts of those he thought might have an eye on the throne. Towards the end of his reign, his fears increased. One of his last acts – on the morning of his death – was to order the execution of an astrologer who had been specially summoned from Germany to interpret a series of menacing omens – and whose answers had obviously been too close to the truth!

Hadrian (AD 117–138) held a sort of *soirée* on the first day of each year, at which he would predict events in the coming year in considerable detail, finally including the hour of his own death. The last of the great emperors, Marcus Aurelius (AD 160–180), consulted astrologers about the association of his wife Faustina with a gladiator, whose muscles she had evidently been admiring from less than a stadium's length away; this same emperor seems also to have kept 'an Egyptian magician' (probably an astrologer) at court.

Above: The Egyptian Zodiac (c. 30 BC) from Denderah. This is the earliest known representation of a Zodiac.

Left: Augustus' ruling planet was Saturn. The Saturnalia devoted to the worship of the planet-god was among the liveliest of Roman festivals: presents were exchanged and slaves attended by their masters.

ASTROLOGY IN THE MIDDLE AGES

A Science of Monks and Noblemen

Astrology has always flourished in a civilized setting. After the fall of Rome and the onset of the Dark Ages the science suffered an eclipse. In the monasteries, however, some interest survived and serious study continued in the Middle East, where Albumasar (805–85), a celebrated Arab astrologer, wrote that 'Only by observing the great diversity of planetary motions can we comprehend the unnumbered varieties of change in this world.'

Gradually, as Europe crept once more towards the light, astrology began to return to man's consciousness–not only as a means of prediction, but as a means of revealing and explaining. Successive Christian philosophers and writers began to rediscover its virtues. One of the results of this new alliance was that various religions were put under the protection of the planets: Judaism was ruled by Saturn; Islam (being both warlike and sensual) by Venus and Mars; Christianity by Mercury–dominant when in Virgo, the sign of the Virgin Mary.

Among the important thinkers who upheld the astrological theory were Albertus Magnus (c1193–1280), a German philosopher and experimental scientist. He believed that the stars could not influence the soul but that they could certainly exert control over the body, and through it reach the human will. Albertus' pupil Thomas Aquinas (1225–74) carried on the debate and went even further than his master, when he made his declaration that 'The celestial bodies are the cause of all that takes place in the sublunar world.'

ASTROLOGY BECOMES A SOCIAL SUCCESS

By the fourteenth century, astrology was firmly established in the universities, supported by theology on the one hand and science on the other. In many noble families the horoscopes of newly-born children were drawn up as a matter of course, and their lives were sometimes dominated by the resulting biographical notes, prepared before they could even walk. There are examples of the horoscopes of favourite horses, and even of pet dogs. Astrology was rapidly becoming all-pervasive, its literature ranging from popular 'Moon books' to serious consideration by both Dante and Chaucer.

Right: These illustrations from a medieval French Book of Hours, set round an early sun dial, show how each sign of the Zodiac was associated with a monthly occupation on the land.

CANCER THE CRAB
Approximately 21 June–22 July. The traditional occupation of this Zodiacal month is cutting grass for haymaking. The labourer uses a scythe; at his belt hangs a sharpening stone.

GEMINI THE TWINS
22 May–20 June. Hunting with hawks and falcons was a favourite seasonal

LEO THE LION
23 July–22 August. This was the time to harvest the wheat, done by hand with a small reaping hook; the wheat was then gathered in sheaves and piled in stooks to dry.

VIRGO THE VIRGIN
23 August–22 September. In the month of the Virgin, when the wheat had dried it was spread out and threshed–also by hand–to separate the grain from the straw.

LIBRA THE SCALES
23 September–22 October. After the grape harvest the grapes were placed in wide, shallow barrels, and crushed by the vineyard workers to extract the juice.

SCORPIO THE SCORPION
23 October–21 November. Sowing for the next

occupation among the landowning classes in the spacious days of the fifteenth century.

TAURUS THE BULL
20 April–21 May. Fertility was once more in the air and people gathered branches and flowers to decorate their streets and houses for the May Day festivities.

ARIES THE RAM
21 March–19 April. In the Zodiacal month of the Ram an important task was to clear away old vines, and trees and bushes were pruned in preparation for the new season.

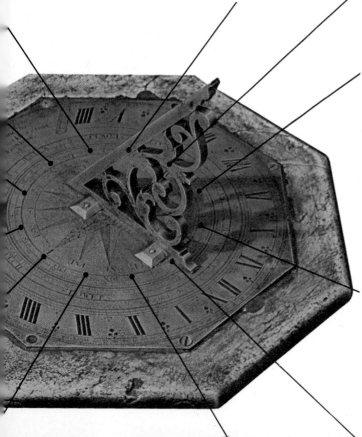

PISCES THE FISHES
19 February–20 March. A time for keeping warm: usually the harsh weather made farming difficult, work slowed and people tended to pass the days relaxing indoors.

AQUARIUS THE WATERBEARER
20 January–18 February. Next came the feasting, an activity watched over in many medieval calendars by two-faced Janus, the ancient Italian god of the month of January.

season often took place under the sign of Scorpio, especially in areas having a clay soil.

SAGITTARIUS THE ARCHER
22 November–21 December. Country people at this time of year knocked down their acorns and sweet chestnuts to fatten their pigs, who had not long to go.

CAPRICORN THE GOAT
22 December–19 January. The pigs and other animals were slaughtered when fodder for them grew scarce, and their carcasses were salted to make the meat last longer.

THE ZODIAC AND THE BODY

How the Twelve Signs Rule our Anatomy

Hugh of St Victor (c 1096–1141), whose philosophy and mysticism were highly influential in the twelfth century, stressed the value of *natural astrology*, which 'deals with the influence of the stars upon our bodily complexions, which vary according to the state of our celestial sphere, as in health and sickness, good and bad weather, fertility and drought'. Even before his time connections were made between the signs of the Zodiac and specific parts of the human body. In the ancient library of Hermes Trismegistus, for example, there appears the notion of correspondences between the macrocosm – the universe – and man: 'The macrocosm embraces the twelve Zodiacal signs and so does man, from his head (the Ram) to his feet, which correspond to the Fishes.'

In recent years astrologers have taken this ancient lore and considered it in the light of modern medical advances. From their researches they have established links between the twelve signs and the glandular and nervous system. These may also be seen to work through what is known as polarity, or the sympathy of opposites. Thus Arian headaches may be related to a kidney condition, the latter falling under the influence of Libra, the opposite sign to Aries. In the captions on these pages the polarity sign appears second.

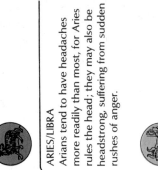

ARIES/LIBRA
Arians tend to have headaches more readily than most, for Aries rules the head; they may also be headstrong, suffering from sudden rushes of anger.

TAURUS/SCORPIO
Taureans are vulnerable to colds and chills, for Taurus rules the throat and neck; it is advisable to keep the throat protected during cold weather.

CANCER/CAPRICORN
Cancerians traditionally tend to worry more than most, and since Cancer rules the stomach their tensions may provoke stomach upsets or even ulcers.

VIRGO/PISCES
Virgo rules the nervous system and intestines, and Virgoans (like Cancerians) tend to suffer from slight stomach upsets, often of a digestive type; many Virgoans are vegetarians, and anyway should watch their diet.

GEMINI/SAGITTARIUS
Geminians may tend to break collar-bones and arms, which are ruled by this sign; they may also find that colds fly immediately to their chests and lungs, and should guard those areas.

SAGITTARIUS/GEMINI

Sagittarians need exercise and the women of this sign should take special care, for they put on weight very easily around the hips and thighs. Sagittarius also rules the liver.

AQUARIUS/LEO

Aquarians playing rough games should watch their shins and ankles; but Aquarius also rules the circulation, and circulatory difficulties (varicose veins, hardening of the arteries) may arise in old age.

PISCES/VIRGO

Anything wrong with a Piscean's feet immediately irritates him; and Piscean feet are often slightly misshapen. Pisceans should also remember that they do not react well to drugs.

LEO/AQUARIUS

Leo's strong association with the heart can in late years mean weakness in that organ, especially if Leo subjects pursue their appetite for the high life and so put too much strain on their hearts.

LIBRA/ARIES

The sign's connection with the kidneys is such that any emotional upset can immediately cause a stomach upset, too; a good reason for controlling the temper!

SCORPIO/TAURUS

Scorpio's association with the sexual organs can lead to impotence in males; more usually the effect is psychological, and Scorpios may be stimulated to violent emotions as well as actions.

CAPRICORN/CANCER

The knees and teeth are emphasized by this sign; dental decay can occur, as can a stiffening of the joints—indeed Capricorn sometimes limits movement by rheumatism.

THE PLANETS AND THE BODY

How the Ten Planets Influence our Glandular System

An important set of correspondences has long existed between specific body areas and the planets. These were used chiefly for medical purposes. Originally they applied to the Sun, Moon and the other five known planets; later they were of course revised to include Uranus, Neptune and Pluto—once the natures of these 'modern' planets could be properly assessed.

A seventeenth-century book, the *Astrological Judgment of Diseases* by Nicholas Culpeper (1616–54), though many astrologers today would not agree with its conclusions, is interesting for its detailed lists of the parts of the body ruled by planets and signs, the diseases ruled by signs and notes on their diagnosis. Culpeper also devised astrological tests to discover whether a patient was faking symptoms, and he sets out a well-reasoned procedure for cure. This includes consideration of the planet governing the disease; side by side with this astrological commentary run purely medical notes dealing with pulse readings, conditions of the blood and urine, and so on.

Since Culpeper, modern medical progress has uncovered a more significant zone of influence—that between the planets and the endocrine glands. These small but vital glands release hormones into the blood and control a great diversity of body functions, from the way we breathe to the expression of our sexual needs.

MERCURY
The brain and nervous system as a whole is ruled by Mercury, which also exerts influence on the way we breathe.

VENUS
The parathyroids, which control the calcium level of the body fluids, are ruled by Venus, which traditionally is connected with the throat, kidneys and lumbar region.

THE SUN
The Sun is particularly associated with the thymus, though it also rules (traditionally) the heart, back and spinal column.

JUPITER
Jupiter's concern is with the liver and its cleansing work; but it also affects the pituitary gland, which regulates hormone growth and production, and governs our physical growth.

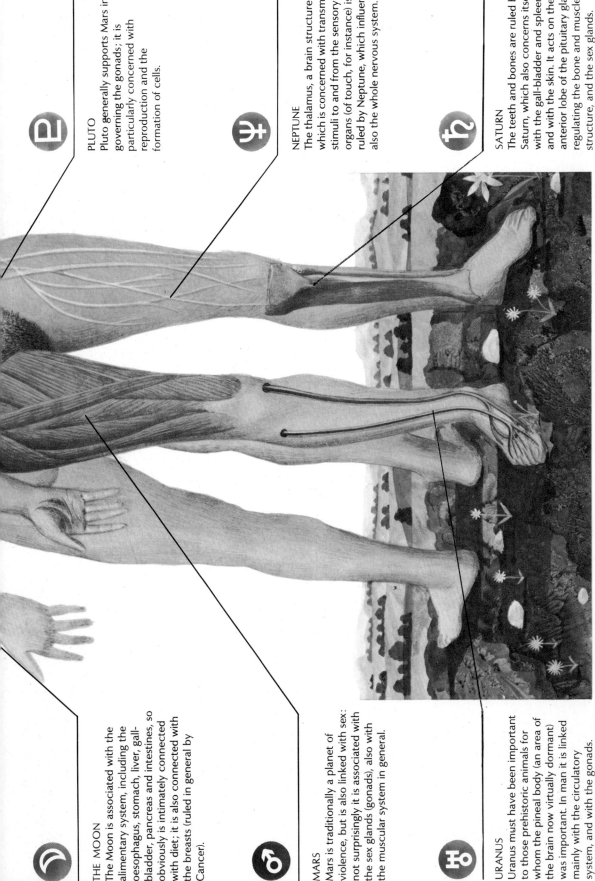

PLUTO
Pluto generally supports Mars in governing the gonads; it is particularly concerned with reproduction and the formation of cells.

NEPTUNE
The thalamus, a brain structure which is concerned with transmitting stimuli to and from the sensory organs (of touch, for instance) is ruled by Neptune, which influences also the whole nervous system.

SATURN
The teeth and bones are ruled by Saturn, which also concerns itself with the gall-bladder and spleen, and with the skin. It acts on the anterior lobe of the pituitary gland, regulating the bone and muscle structure, and the sex glands.

THE MOON
The Moon is associated with the alimentary system, including the oesophagus, stomach, liver, gall-bladder, pancreas and intestines, so obviously is intimately connected with diet; it is also connected with the breasts (ruled in general by Cancer).

MARS
Mars is traditionally a planet of violence, but is also linked with sex: not surprisingly it is associated with the sex glands (gonads), also with the muscular system in general.

URANUS
Uranus must have been important to those prehistoric animals for whom the pineal body (an area of the brain now virtually dormant) was important. In man it is linked mainly with the circulatory system, and with the gonads.

THE SCIENTIFIC REVOLUTION
Copernicus Reshapes the Universe

The influence of astrologers in the sixteenth and seventeenth centuries was at its weightiest in the courts of Europe. Astrology was found to be intellectually stimulating as well as practically useful for the conduct of war and peace, and in politics and private life. Some of the royal advisers were astronomer-astrologers, some had an equal interest in the occult or in alchemy. And so, while Elizabeth I of England summoned the visionary Dr Dee and heard his advice, Catherine de Medici in France was advised by Nostradamus, and Christian IV of Denmark, Sigismund III of Poland (and Sweden) and Frederick of Bohemia all had astrologers attached to their courts.

THE GREAT ASTRONOMERS

One event that caused a great stir was the publication in 1543 by Copernicus, the Polish church official and astronomer, of his new theory of the universe. In it he demolished the sacred idea, held by scientists since Ptolemy's day (c AD 120–180), that the Sun, Moon and planets all revolved around the Earth. Copernicus proposed instead that the Sun lay at the centre. People were horrified, the Church banned his work and it remained on the Papal Index until 1835. But astrological theory was little affected by Copernicus—even when his findings were later confirmed by Johannes Kepler (1571–1630); the reason is that astrology is concerned with the positions of the planets *as seen from* Earth; for purposes of calculation it was not unreasonable to maintain the Earth at the centre of the universe.

The great astronomers of the period were attached to the courts of various European rulers, and invariably were also astrologers. Indeed Tycho Brahe (1546–1601) in his *De disciplinus mathematicus* states that 'those who deny the influence of the planets violate clear evidence which for educated people of sound judgment it is not suitable to contradict'. And Kepler, who was Brahe's successor as Imperial Mathematician at the court of the Holy Roman Emperor, wrote in *De stella nova:* 'Nothing exists nor happens in the visible sky that is not sensed in some hidden moment by the faculties of Earth and Nature.'

It would be wrong to assume that all thinking men of this period believed completely in astrology as a means of accurate prediction. This would be an over-statement. The general attitude was nearer that of Francis Bacon (1561–1626). 'I am certain,' he wrote, 'that the celestial bodies have in them certain influences besides heat and light.' His cautious view underlines the growing scientific spirit among intelligent men of the day.

Left: In these star maps drawn by G. C. Eimmart the constellations of the Zodiac are grouped along the ecliptic, or path of the Sun, at the base of each hemisphere. Around the main charts diagrams explain the phases of the Moon (*bottom left*), the seasons (*bottom right*) and the tides (*top right*); the others describe three different universal systems. In that of Ptolemy (*top centre*) the Earth lies at the centre of the universe, while Copernicus (*bottom centre*) placed the Sun at the core of his system; and Tycho Brahe (*top left*) put the Earth in the centre but made the planets orbit the Sun.

THE MECHANICAL COSMOS
Rational Science and the Rebirth of Astrology

Towards the end of the seventeenth century astrology fell from general favour. Some people assume that the publication in 1687 of Isaac Newton's *Principia* began this process. On the contrary, astrological practices had begun to deteriorate some years before that date. There had always been dishonest practitioners on the edge of the subject, ready to take advantage of the over-credulous. Now they multiplied as they saw that the middle classes, gradually becoming more educated, offered a rich ground for speculators who claimed impossible powers of prediction.

The seventeenth century was, above all, the age of science and rationalism. Since the first telescopic observations, made by Harriott, Galileo and Marius in about 1609–10, there was a general dedication to scientific truths. A rift occurred between astrology, which depends not only on mathematics but on intuition and sensitivity as well, and those areas of knowledge in which it was permissible to verify new theories only by empirical means. Ironically however, Isaac Newton himself, the man whose book finally opened the modern phase of astronomy, never lost his profound regard for the hidden truths of astrology.

ASTROLOGY TURNS THE CORNER

During the nineteenth century there were few astrologers with a serious interest in their craft, and where astrology flourished it was usually debased by occultism. Astrological magazines such as *The Prophetic Messenger* published predictions and information about magic talismans and 'animal magnetism', and were far from being serious astrological publications. But, towards the end of the century, astrology began to revive under the aegis of Madame Blavatsky and the Theosophists. Later William Frederick Allan (1860–1917) under the nom-de-plume of 'Alan Leo' became the first important popular astrologer of the twentieth century; although the mass-produced horoscopes he sent out to the public at large were of little value, his textbooks on astrology were responsibly written and are still read for their instructional value in the 1970s.

In the USA the first popular astrologer of importance was Evangeline Adams (1865–1930), whose remarkable predictions brought her fame and a dedicated following. She is best remembered for her radio series, which did much to publicize the benefits of astrology. In more recent years Dane Rudhyar (1895–   ) has sought to bring astrology to a high academic level, investing it with a language by which 'man can discover the pattern of order which reveals both his individuality and his destiny'. In Europe, meanwhile, many people were swayed by the astrological essays of C. G. Jung (1875–1961).

Today, of course, astrology is becoming an essential part of our culture and is making a widely respected contribution in many fields, including those of business, psychiatry, science, education, and the law. Astrology has done more than come in out of the cold. It is now a major source of warmth to many thousands of people.

Above is an orrery, a mechanical device that demonstrates the relative motions of the celestial bodies. This example was made in 1794 and shows the Sun in the centre: around it turn Mercury (white disk), Venus, the Earth and the Moon.

The changing cosmic intensity of the double star Algol: its brightness decreases (1 and 3) when the fainter star eclipses its partner; but when (2 and 4) the brighter member is to the fore the combined body emits more light.

Above: The Trifid Nebula in Sagittarius. Modern research suggests that the rhythms of bodies remote in space may be linked by a complex system of harmonies to man's own activity cycles such as our heartbeats and brain rhythms.

Left: The light-curve diagram below shows how emissions from the double star Algol vary every 2½ days. Scientists are now considering whether such cosmic activities may affect our lives on Earth.

THE NEW ASTROLOGY

Exploring the Frontiers of Cosmic Energy

Today, in the celebrated words of the great psychologist C. G. Jung, astrology 'knocks at the doors of the universities, from which it was banished some three hundred years ago'. Every year astrologers meet at international conferences to exchange information and discuss new developments which link astrology with all manner of scientific disciplines. Doctors, for example, find astrology useful: in Czechoslovakia, Dr. Eugen Jonas has been experimenting in the prediction of the sex of unborn children, and has also produced impressive evidence to show that fertility in women fluctuates with the motions of the Sun and Moon.

Meteorologists are becoming more and more aware of the effect the planets have on terrestrial weather—producing statistics to show that the Moon influences rainfall, Mercury the temperature, and the planetary cycles the general year-to-year weather picture. Dr. R. Tomaschek, Chairman of the World Geophysical Council, found the position of Uranus significant in the cases of 134 earthquakes which he studied.

TOWARDS ANCIENT BELIEFS

In Renaissance times, every educated man believed in astrology—that the planets, while not dictating what he *must* do, inclined him to certain actions or attitudes. After three hundred years during which belief tended to swing away, more and more people are now beginning to come to the conclusion that the astrologers are probably right. And science is beginning, slowly, to support the view. As Sir Bernard Lovell, the English astronomer, put it some years ago, 'It almost seems as though we are moving through a series of scientific fantasies to a proof of ancient beliefs.'

In Russia, astrology, like religion, is officially denigrated; in India, perhaps men rely on it too much. In the Western countries in general, public opinion is turning more and more towards the belief that, as Jung wrote, 'whatever is born or done this moment, has the qualities of this moment of time'.

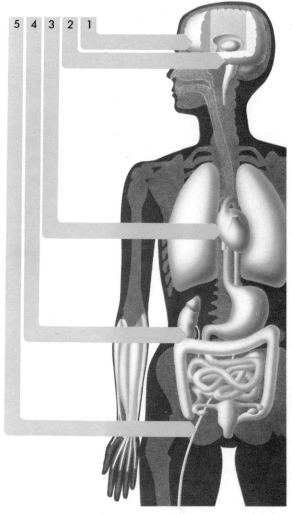

Above: Some of the human activity cycles that may correspond to broader cosmic functions. Beta rhythms (1) affect our sense of judgment; alpha rhythms (2) are most active during sleep; the others shown here relate to the heart (3), the kidneys (4) and the ovaries (5).

Left: We now know that extra-terrestrial powers, especially from the Sun and Moon, affect all kinds of plant and animal behaviour, from oysters and birds to man himself. This diagram shows F. A. Brown Jr's discovery that flatworms (*planetaria*) are directed by lunar phases: at the new Moon (black disk) they turn about 10° to the left on leaving their enclosures; at the time of the full Moon (white disk) they turn to the right by the same amount.

Dr Eugen Jonas wrote that women became fertile at times dictated by the Sun and Moon; and that at conception the Moon in a positive (plus) sign meant the child would be a boy; negative meant a girl.

HOW ASTROLOGY WORKS

The Mechanics of Celestial Knowledge

KEY
A Path of ecliptic
B The fixed Zodiac
C Earth
N/S Poles of the celestial equator

To early man the celestial bodies—chiefly the Sun—were forces to be reckoned with: they had the power to intervene in his life. On the other hand he was reluctant to concede that any external body was more important than the Earth itself, around which the rest of the universe was seen to revolve.

AN EARTH-CENTRED VIEW OF THE UNIVERSE

The celestial sphere, opposite, demonstrates both these ancient attitudes. Today we all know that really the Sun not the Earth lies at the centre of the universe, but modern astrologers, like their ancestors, are principally concerned with the positions of the planets *as seen from* Earth, and so the convention can be retained.

The celestial sphere shows how we might look out from Earth at the universe beyond. There in the sky are the Sun, Moon and planets, all moving within the Zodiacal band against the starry background. This, in astrology, is divided into twelve equal segments (the signs) which serve as reference points for charting the positions taken up by the planets in their various orbits.

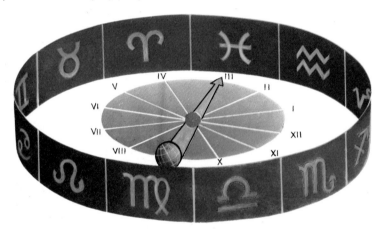

Above: The Sun through the year. Although it is really the Earth that turns round the Sun once a year, to us on Earth it seems to be the Sun that moves. Behind the Sun the fixed signs of the Zodiac—each of which occupies a 30° segment of the band—change from month to month; the Sun is seen, for example, against Pisces during March, the third month of the year.

Below: In addition to the Sun nine other significant astrological bodies—planets—occupy our Solar System. Except for Pluto these always remain within the area of the Zodiac. They are shown below with their ancient glyphs or symbols: these represent, from left to right, Neptune, Saturn, Mars, Venus, the Sun, Mercury, the Moon (next to the Sun in importance), Jupiter, Uranus and Pluto.

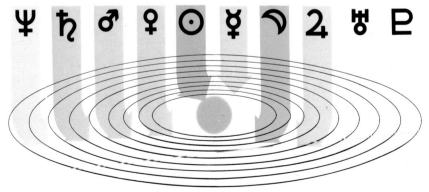

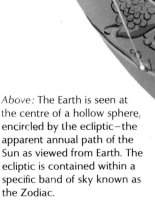

Above: The Earth is seen at the centre of a hollow sphere, encircled by the ecliptic—the apparent annual path of the Sun as viewed from Earth. The ecliptic is contained within a specific band of sky known as the Zodiac.

N

S

B

C

B

A

THE PLANETS

Their Scale, Orbital Paths and Range of Influence

Many who are discovering astrology for the first time may not realize that the Sun, although of the first importance, is not the only active force in the heavens. In serious astrology a subject's Birth Chart is calculated for his or her birth date, time and place, and interpreted according to the positions of *all* the planets. Anyone wishing, incidentally, to see which signs of the Zodiac were occupied by all the planets at his or her birth should consult an ephemeris, or table of planetary positions, for the year of birth.

These positions are determined by precise factors. Although to the ancient Babylonians the planets were known as 'wanderers' or 'goats' because they seemed to move erratically across the sky—in contrast to the 'fixed' stars that were so far away as to seem unmoving—in fact the planets are held by gravity to a fairly regular course around the Sun.

The Sun is the major body of the Solar System, in which we live. In size it is enormous: it has a diameter of 865,000 miles and its volume is more than a million times greater than the Earth's. Gravity of course works by mass rather than size: the greater the mass the greater the pull one body exerts on another. At times this can cause one planet physically to influence another, setting up 'perturbations' or irregular movements. This was precisely what led to the discovery of Pluto in 1930, as we shall see.

THE ASTROLOGER'S VIEW

In astrology the Sun and Moon are regarded as planets. In addition to them, eight other bodies in the Solar System are held to be astrologically significant. Those nearest to the Sun—Mercury, Venus, Mars, Jupiter and Saturn—were known in ancient times and each early acquired a set of human characteristics and was associated with such earthly phenomena as a specific metal, a precious stone, and so on. Each, furthermore, had a special relationship with at least one sign of the Zodiac. The Sun and Moon ruled one sign each and the other planets two signs each.

THE MODERN PLANETS

When Uranus, the nearest of the three modern planets, was discovered by William Herschel in 1781, astrologers had to reassess these Zodiacal relationships. After a great deal of consideration—and not a little controversy—Uranus was felt to represent the principle of sudden, disruptive change and was allied to Aquarius (which formerly had been felt to reflect certain qualities of Saturn).

A similar process followed the appearance of Neptune in 1846. This planet was linked with Pisces since they were felt to share qualities of receptivity and diffuseness. Pluto, the latest planet, is very new. It was discovered only in 1930, when irregularities in the motions of Uranus and Neptune suggested to scientists that a third body, by its gravitational pull, was influencing their orbital pattern. Dramatically, a team led by Clyde Tombaugh at the Lowell Observatory in Arizona proved this to be the case—and the tenth planet was added to astrological lore.

Today most astrologers agree with the association of Pluto, whose keyword is 'elimination', with Scorpio. They are, all the same, very aware of the strong residual influence of Mars in that sign.

Because of their remoteness the three modern planets move very slowly through the Zodiac. Many astrologers believe that their influence is similarly 'distant', extending over entire generations rather than closely affecting individual lives as, in particular, the Sun does.

Left: The signs and their ruling planets. These are: Sun–Leo; Moon–Cancer; Mercury–Gemini, Virgo; Venus–Taurus, Libra; Mars–Aries; Jupiter–Sagittarius; Saturn–Capricorn; Uranus–Aquarius; Neptune–Pisces, and Pluto–Scorpio. The old links, i.e. before the discovery of the modern planets, are shown in white.

Right and below: The planets are seen extending outwards from the fierce heat of the Sun to the cold, remote zone occupied by Uranus, Neptune and Pluto; and in scale against part of the Sun's curvature with their glyphs (the Moon is not shown).

MERCURY   VENUS   EAR

MARS   JUPITER   SATURN   URANUS   NEPTUNE   PLUTO

PLANET PEOPLE

How the Planets Can Dominate Our Lives

You probably know your Sun-sign: that you have, say, the Sun in Cancer (if you were born between 21 June–22 July); but until you either ask an astrologer to work it out, or learn to work it out for yourself, you will not know which signs of the Zodiac the other planets occupy. Quite often another planet makes its presence felt very strongly indeed on an individual's personality, showing characteristics that are different to those of the Sun sign. Here are some examples of very powerful influences by planets on people—influences which have made a vital mark on their personalities.

THE SUN

KEYWORD: POWER

Our two Sun people both, as it happens, had the Sun rising in Gemini. In Queen Victoria's case, this made her in essence a very 'queenly' person—almost adding an element of Leo to her personality

(the Sun rules Leo). The second Sun person is Richard Wagner: the huge scale of his operas and of his whole artistic expression are characteristic of what astrologers would call 'a prominent Sun'. Being in Gemini, it gave him considerable duality—he wrote the libretti as well as the music of his operas.

THE MOON

KEYWORDS: RESPONSE, FLUCTUATION

The significance of the Moon in a Birth Chart is second only to that of the Sun; and when it is in its own sign (Cancer), or in certain other special positions, its characteristics can be almost over-

whelmingly powerful. Lord Byron had a very powerful Moon in Cancer—and this made personal relationships difficult for him. The famous conductor Arturo Toscanini also had a prominent Moon; it represented for him the general public, and his fame, as well as his dealings with his orchestra as a whole.

MERCURY

KEYWORD: COMMUNICATION

Among the characteristics of Aquarius are originality, eccentricity, inventiveness: Jules Verne had Mercury in this sign, in the area of his Chart influencing his career. Mercury represents the

mind, writing and communication, and all the originality and futuristic qualities of Aquarius were combined with those of Mercury in Verne's science fiction.

VENUS

KEYWORD: HARMONY

The Venus in Isadora Duncan's Chart was very powerful. It was in Aries, which is a very assertive sign; those with important planets in it are usually

highly sexed. The romantic side of Venus was very strong in Isadora, and many of her real needs were also Venus-influenced—her need, for example, to be loved, and to give both love and affection.

SATURN

KEYWORD: LIMITATION

Saturn in George Gershwin's Chart was in Sagittarius when he was born, and fell in the area of his Chart concerned with his health. It undoubtedly undermined his physical strength; Gershwin died at the relatively early age of thirty-nine, two years after completing the opera, *Porgy and Bess*. The Saturn in Pablo Picasso's Chart is also interesting—it is in Taurus, and its influence is particularly strong in the work Picasso did at the time of the Spanish Civil War: the important painting *Guernica* is a striking example, as are some of the passionately expressive sculptures that he created.

JUPITER

KEYWORD: EXPANSION

Albert Einstein had a marvellous Jupiter in his Birth Chart: it fell in Aquarius, the humanitarian sign. Jupiter was also in the area of his Chart ruling the mind in its most advanced and broadest capacity. Jupiter worked in a different way for the notorious spy Mata Hari. She had the planet rising in the secretive, emotional water sign, Scorpio, and her Jupiter principle of expansiveness only came decisively to the fore when, facing the firing-squad, she thanked the officer commanding her execution.

MARS

KEYWORDS: ENERGY, INITIATIVE
Horatio Viscount Nelson had a very prominent Mars in his Birth Chart. It was rising in Scorpio when he was born. This gave him fantastic powers of endurance, an abundance of emotional energy and bravery. Vincent van Gogh also had an important Mars, but in his case it was in the less intense sign, Pisces. Sacrifice is very much a part of the Piscean influence, and the fact that van Gogh cut off his ear could easily be related to this planet's influence, for Mars is a violent planet and can lead people to take impulsive action under pressure.

THE MODERN PLANETS

The three modern planets—Uranus, Neptune and Pluto—are so far away that they travel very slowly along the ecliptic. Whereas the Sun moves once through the Zodiac or 360° in a year, Uranus moves approximately 4°, Neptune 2° and Pluto 1°. Thus Uranus takes seven years to pass through one sign of the Zodiac (30°), while Neptune takes fourteen years and Pluto—because it has an eccentric orbit—anything from thirteen to thirty-two years. The modern planets will therefore occupy similar positions in the Birth Charts of people born over an extended period; and for this reason their influences are believed to be over generations more than individuals—unless, of course, one of these planets is sensitively placed in a Chart. This could be because it is 'in aspect' (having a specific angular relationship) with another planet or group of planets; in which case the modern planet must be assessed together with the aspected planet(s) and their combined effect carefully weighed.

URANUS

KEYWORD: SUDDEN CHANGE
Franklin D. Roosevelt had Uranus accentuated in his Chart; as with Gershwin's Saturn, it fell in the area of the Chart concerning health. Uranus is related to paralysis, which crippled Roosevelt for most of his active political career. Karl Marx was also a Uranian person: in him the Uranian qualities of radicalism and humanitarianism were very powerfully expressed. His whole life centred around these ideals.

NEPTUNE

KEYWORD: CLOUDINESS
The influence of the planet Neptune is various: at its best it can make a true and inspired actor, poet or artist, but under other circumstances it can lead to suicidal tendencies. Marilyn Monroe had all the splendid attributes of Neptune (which include glamour as well as artistic ability) but the negative side of the planet's influence proved tragically strong. Neptune was extremely powerfully placed in her Chart and was astrologically 'afflicted'—meaning that other planets occupied difficult relationships to it, making her liable at times to commit extreme actions.

PLUTO

KEYWORD: ELIMINATION
Pluto's influence is generally believed by astrologers to be disruptive: it can play havoc in many ways with the unconscious, while at its best it can help people to make fresh starts in life, or to live through drastic periods of upheaval, coming through well or badly according to the planet's position in the Chart and its relationships to other planets. The Pluto in Marlene Dietrich's Chart falls in the area concerned with overseas countries and, many believe has brought about her worldwide fame. Another very interesting Pluto person is Greta Garbo. The influence of her Pluto has been the reverse of Dietrich's case, for it falls in the area of her Chart relating to seclusion and withdrawal. Garbo disappeared from the public eye in 1941, and has stayed in seclusion ever since. Some have affirmed that Pluto played a key part in this drastic change.

THE USES OF ASTROLOGY

Eight ways to Deepen Your Experience of Life

'But how can astrology help *me*?' The question is a very natural one—especially if you have never had the experience of reading a full astrological report. The answer is that if your full Birth Chart is consulted by a professional astrologer there will be no area of your everyday life in which he or she cannot be of help to you. Here are just a few.

KNOWING YOURSELF

You may think that you know as much about yourself as you want to! But astrology can reveal, in advance, the days when you may be feeling strangely impatient, the days when your temper may be snappy, the days when you will be feeling particularly relaxed. It can tell you some of the things your best friends might hesitate to reveal: that you can be selfish or that your eating habits may bring a weight problem.

CAREERS

If you are just leaving school or college, an astrologer can provide a list of careers in which you may be interested; or if you feel restless, and want a change of occupation, you can learn from him whether in fact it is a good time for such a change, and the direction in in which you might like to lead your life. And of course you can ask an astrologer about careers for your children.

CHILDREN

Career advice is only one area of work an astrologer can do for children: even with very young children, he can tell you when they may go through that worrying stage of infant illnesses—mumps, chickenpox, and so on. He can suggest what sort of school would best suit *your* child's temperament; and which parent is best suited to dealing with the different areas of the child's personality. The child may, for example, turn to his mother in times of difficulty but perhaps he enjoys the company of his father more when the family goes out for the day.

SEX AND LOVE

In synastry, a term for the comparison of Birth Charts, the astrologer assesses just how suited two people

are to each other. Not that he will tell you not to marry the girl! But he can point out that while you like peace and quiet, she really feels at her best at a noisy party; that while you tend to throw your money around, she prefers to save it. After that it's up to you to decide. However, in every marriage there are difficult times and an astrologer will not only see such problem periods approaching, he will also be able to say whether a permanent break is likely or just a temporary hitch.

BUSINESS

Many businessmen now consult astrologers about the best time to make heavy investments, to sell overseas, to make a takeover bid . . . and an astrologer will be able to warn a businessman of a period when he may be particularly under stress, and would do better to take some time off.

HEALTH

Some of the most valuable work an astrologer can do is in warning clients of periods when their health may be a little low, when they may tend to catch cold, or feel run-down and should take a tonic. Using traditional astrology, it is also possible to warn which areas of the body may be weak, and should be specially watched and checked by a doctor—and at what times this is likely to happen.

WEATHER

Ask an astrologer what the weather is going to be like in California or New South Wales, Algiers or Boston, during the third week in May. A practised astrological weather forecaster will be much more accurate than a meteorologist (some astrologers have records of 87% accuracy in this field).

FOR THE FUN OF IT!

Astrology is fun, too; use it to choose the colour of gift wrapping paper, or to choose the gift inside; use it to make up a dinner-table of guests, or to choose a pet. And always remember that it is nothing to do with 'fate': you still have free will. Astrology doesn't tell you what *will* happen, what you *must* do. It's like a weather-forecast: if rain is likely, you can always stay indoors!

Astrologers are often asked to interpret the birth data of couples planning to marry. Either singly or compared, the Charts can reveal much about character and compatibility that many prefer to know *before* the shoes and rice. After that it's up to them—and to love—to make the most of each other.

YOU AND YOUR ASTROLOGER

First Steps in Complete Astro-analysis

Consulting an astrologer is a fascinating and revealing experience for anyone. Whether you are in need of help—perhaps with a difficult emotional or career problem—or whether you simply want to find out more about yourself and your psychological motivation you will, after the consultation or the arrival of a written report, be in a much better position to face life with greater confidence.

The first thing an astrologer must do before he can help you is to take your birth date, time and place. From these he calculates the positions of all the planets in their various signs of the Zodiac and houses (see page 22) for that given moment and location. He in fact makes a map of the sky, one which is very individual to *you*; no two people can have the same Birth Chart (as the map is called) unless they were born at precisely the same moment in the same hospital or street—for the whole celestial picture changes every four minutes for every location on earth.

First contact with an astrologer often comes when a fresh approach is needed to an emotional problem, perhaps some kind of marital deadlock.

If you do, incidentally, meet someone who was born within the same hour and in the same area as yourself—and whose chart is very similar if not identical to yours—you may be astounded by the similarities between your life and that of your 'astrological twin'. You may well share personal mannerisms and pursue the same careers and pastimes—you may even marry each other, it has been known!

From the Birth Chart the astrologer is able to build up a picture of you—your motivation, your potential, how you react in emotional relationships, and so on. As you grow older, so your Birth Chart grows older with you, and by studying the positions of the planets for, say, eighteen days after you were born (known as 'progressing' the Chart) the astrologer is able to assess the trends which were working in your life when you were eighteen years old. He also studies the planets as

they appear in the sky at the present time, and relates their positions to the positions they occupied at the time of your birth.

People unhappy in their work find impartial advice hard to come by and many turn to astrology for expert and impartial guidance on how best to use their real talents.

Do not expect your astrologer to tell you that you will fall in love with a beautiful blonde on 26 October, and marry her three weeks later! Serious astrologers do not predict events: they are not fortune-tellers. They assess the trends working in their clients' lives, and will say such things as: 'You may live through a blissfully happy and romantic period', or, 'There is indication of an important period of change, likely to concern your career'; *never* 'This (or that) *will* happen'.

Remember, too, that it takes a good astrologer many days to study and fully interpret a Birth and Progressed Chart; if he offers a too-rapid service, the quality of his service may well be found wanting. No, wait until you are in a position to consult a reputable astrologer; you will be all the more satisfied with the results, and richer in knowledge of yourself.

Responsible astrologers advise on trends but make no firm predictions. They cannot foresee death but they can help a client's health by anticipating moments of stress.

INDEX

Page numbers in italics refer to illustrations

ASTROLOGICAL ORGANIZATIONS

The American Federation of Astrologers (Robert W. Cooper, Executive Secretary), 6 Library Court, Capitol Hill, Washington D.C. 20003.

The Astrological Association (Charles Harvey D.F.Astrol.S., Hon. Secretary), 36 Tweedy Road, Bromley, Kent BR1 3PP, England.

The Faculty of Astrological Studies (The Secretary), 37 Campden Hill Towers, London W11 3QW, England.

ACKNOWLEDGEMENTS

Editor Michael Leitch, Art Director Peter Kindersley, Designed by Martin Bronkhorst with Nick Eddison

The Planetary and Zodiac Library features work by the following artists: Donna Brown, Graham Brownridge,

Carol Binch, Bryony Dahl, Barry Evans, Andrew Farmer, Harry Hants, Chris McKewan, Ian Miller, Brian Palmer, William Rankin, Justin Todd, Paul Webb.
Other illustrations appearing in this series were kindly supplied by the

Bodleian Library, Oxford, British Museum, Bob Cundy, C. M. Dixon, Michael Holford, Mansell Collection, Picturepoint, Science Museum, London, and Roger Viollet. Picture research by Ann Davies and Anne Horton.